Mysteries of Seaweed

QUESTIONS AND ANSWERS

Gilbert Newton

DEDICATION

This book is dedicated to the memory of Dr. Imre Friedmann whose botany class at Florida State University introduced me to the wonderful world of seaweeds.

Published by Gilbert Newton
gdnewton@comcast.net

ISBN 978-0-9978182-9-1

This book produced by Nancy Viall Shoemaker, West Barnstable Press
www.westbarnstablepress.com

Foreword

As scientist, environmental activist, teacher, and author, Gil Newton offers us a window into the world of nature.

For 36 years Gil brought science to the children of the Sandwich, Mass. school system; he developed the STEM (Science, Technology, Engineering, Mathematics) Academy as its Director.

To watch Mr. Newton teach is to witness joy. As a native Cape Codder, his focus of study is the flora and fauna of coastal seas and lands; he is happiest when he shares the knowledge he has acquired over the last five decades. Gil also applies his skill of instruction at Cape Cod Community College and Massachusetts Maritime Academy.

I have had the pleasure of working with Gil on six books as his editor and designer. Each publication has been carefully crafted from his study of the beautiful and exciting life that blooms and thrives where land meets sea. His comprehension of the complexity of nature's interdependence is astounding as is his ability to explain nature's water-side systems.

His newest book, *Mysteries of Seaweed: Questions and Answers*, is the result of decades of study, field work, and teaching. Gil has taken hundreds, maybe thousands of students to the shores of Cape Cod and New England, explaining the difference between codium and rockweed, the life cycle of sea lettuce, and the elaborate system of coastal plants and animals. He has listened to his students' questions. This book is a reply to those questions.

I never stop learning from Gil.

Nancy Viall Shoemaker

Introduction

For many years I have been teaching classes and giving presentations on the topic of seaweeds, one of my areas of research in graduate school – and a life-long interest. Since my field guide *Seaweeds of Cape Cod Shores* was published, I have been very busy sharing my passion with others for this fascinating group of marine life.

At the end of each talk or class, I am asked many follow-up questions. Over the years, these inquiries have accumulated to the point that I have started inserting additional information into my presentations. I write down people's questions to help me improve my talks. Some of the best questions have come when I lead groups to examine algae in their natural environments at the beach or the salt marsh.

This book is a collection of these questions and many important sets of information about seaweeds that curious explorers of the seashore want to know. There is no particular order to these questions. Readers can scan the questions and check out the answers that interest them. I'm sure that as time goes on more questions will arise and I'm sorry if I've left out any that the reader may have.

I am often asked at my presentations how I became interested in seaweeds. I grew up on Cape Cod and spent many hours exploring the seashore trying to identify as many marine species as I could. My main interests at that time were the animals. However I could not help but notice the seaweeds as well. As a biology major in college, I was required to take a botany class so I registered for one entitled "Nonvascular Plant Morphology." Seaweeds were still considered plants at that time. On the first day of class the professor had us draw and write down information on dozens of algae specimens lined up on the lab benches.

I didn't get very far before becoming quickly fascinated with the specimens on display. There were algae of bright colors, complicated life cycles, and unusual shapes. Some resembled little statues covered in lime. Others looked like paint brushes or small cups. And there was one that resembled a cluster of small grapes.

I wanted to learn more about this beautiful group of living organisms - and so I began my studies that continue today. The scientific study of algae (phycology) progresses with new areas of understanding and research every day, particularly in the growing interest of seaweed as commercial and industrial products. Their ecological significance is now more widely understood and appreciated. And one must not overlook the fact that seaweeds are also beautiful in their variable designs, shapes and colors. I hope the following questions and answers, along with the photographs, will inspire others to discover and learn more about these ancient inhabitants of the sea.

Gil Newton

NVS

Questions
AND
Answers

What kind of plants are seaweeds?

Technically, seaweeds are not true plants. Though they have chlorophyll and can photosynthesize like plants, they lack the conducting structures known as vascular tissue (xylem and phloem) that plants have. Seaweeds are placed in the kingdom Protista and do not have true leaves, stems, roots, flowers, fruits or seeds. Many seaweed structures resemble these plant parts but have different names. Thus, we describe an alga's leaf-like blade, its stem-like stipe, and its root-like holdfast. Some, such as *Sargassum*, have small berry-like structures which are air bladders and help the alga float to the surface. A few species of brown and red algae contain specialized conducting cells such as the trumpet hyphae in kelp.

Are there any poisonous seaweeds?

Some seaweeds contain toxins that can affect the growth of coral. Other species grow in areas of nitrogen runoff, indicating the presence of sewage which may contain pollutants that are absorbed by the seaweed. Some seaweeds have been known to concentrate harmful contaminants such as mercury or arsenic. One seaweed, *Desmerestia*, contains sulfuric acid in its vacuoles. This is considered an adaptation to prevent consumption by herbivores.

Is sea lettuce edible?

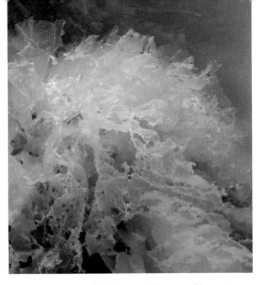

Ulva lactuca, the sea lettuce, is used in seasoning, particularly in soups and salads. It can also be consumed directly and is a source of most vitamins including vitamin B-12, C and E. It is a good source of protein, iodine, potassium and iron. However, sea lettuce is a nitrogen-loving species and often grows abundantly in bays and estuaries where there is sewage and road runoff.

What is the largest seaweed?

The giant bladder kelp (*Macrocystis pyrifera*) grows along the Pacific coast and is particularly abundant in California. This brown seaweed can grow up to 150 feet long and forms dense populations or "forests" along the coastline. These kelp forests are diverse ecosystems that support over 1,000 marine animal species. Their upper fronds form an extensive canopy which is harvested as a source of algin widely used in many commercial food products.

Why is Codium considered a nuisance alga?

Codium fragile is an introduced and highly invasive plant along the northeastern Atlantic coast. The young alga can attach to practically any hard surface. *Codium* can damage shellfish beds by growing over the filter-feeding siphons of clams and blocking their ability to feed. It can also weigh down the mobile scallops, preventing them from feeding. *Codium* is spongy and buoyant and can remove shellfish from their natural habitat by floating away with a clam or snail still attached. *Codium* can also grow so thick that it blocks sunlight to eelgrass in subtidal waters, thus reducing the ability of the eelgrass to photosynthesize and provide food to the numerous animals that live there.

What is mung?

Mung is a population bloom of the brown alga *Pylaiella* and the related *Ectocarpus*. It occurs during the warmest months of summer and can be a major nuisance along the shore by entangling fishermen's nets and interfering with swimmers. *Pylaiella* and *Ectocarpus* are filamentous brown algae genera that have a slimy texture and can grow in shallow water.
There is speculation that its incidence is increasing due to nitrogen loading but it may also be related to ocean currents that transport the algae from one area to another.

How long do seaweeds live?

The lifespan of seaweeds varies with different species. There are some annual seaweeds that only live for a few weeks such as the common sea lettuce (*Ulva lactuca*). Other species such as the knotted wrack (*Ascophyllum nodosum*) may live for more than two decades. But it's much more complicated than that. Several algae species exhibit different stages throughout the year known as an alternation of generations. Some undergo a microscopic stage before growing into a visible thallus.

What is Kombu?

Kombu comes from kelps, particularly *Laminaria*, and is used as either a powder or strips after drying. Kelps are valuable seaweeds and are used as stabilizers in dairy products and supplements in baked goods and processed foods. The substance extracted is alginate which is widely used in these

NVS

and other commercial products. Kombu stock is a common component of many Japanese recipes≠– in soups and the preparation of fish.

5

What are kelps and how are they important?

Kelp is a collective term for several large brown algae species such as *Laminaria* and *Macrocystis*. They are economically significant because of the substance alginate (which is extracted from the blades) and are used as a stabilizer and thickener in many food products including salad dressings, condiments such as mustard, ice cream, puddings, and beer. Kelp seaweeds are important primary producers along the Atlantic and Pacific coastlines, producing oxygen and food for a large diversity of animals. The animal species in the kelp forests find shelter and food among the kelp blades. Kelp beds are also important nurseries for larvae and eggs of several species.

Gil Newton

Can seaweed be used as a biofuel?

Certain seaweeds such as sugar kelp (*Laminaria saccharina*) can be farmed and cultivated on a large scale. Offshore seaweed farms could produce enough material to support a biofuel program that can supplement transportation needs. In time this could even replace corn as a biofuel. Many believe corn production should be used as a food source instead of fuel. There are some red algae species that could also be harvested as a biofuel.

NVS

What is the seaweed wrap around sushi?

This seaweed is called nori (*Porphyra*) and is a multi-billion dollar industry throughout Asia and other parts of the world. Nori is a very nutritious product, rich in vitamins, proteins, minerals and carbohydrates. For example, it has a high con-centration of vitamin C. It has been used as a food product for centuries and its reddish-purple blades are harvested from large nets in shallow water. *Porphyra* also has a microscopic stage (Conchocellis) in which algae spores are attached to rocks and shells. The blades are thin and may be a few inches across. It can be purchased in health food stores in the United States in a dried form.

Are different seaweeds at different depths?

Most marine algae species are distributed in specific zones depending on the wavelength of light that is absorbed by the pigments in their cells. For example, red algae are usually found in deeper water because they absorb blue light. Many brown algae species are in a zone just below mean low water. These algae also need a strong substrate for attachment. In general the distribution of marine algae starts with the green algae in the upper intertidal zone followed by brown algae just below the low tide mark, and then the red algae in the lower zones.

Are there seaweeds that grow mainly in the winter?

Two brown algae cold water species, *Scytosiphon lomentaria* and *Petalonia fascia*, often grow together in the water. *Scytosiphon*, also called the sausage alga is characterized by periodic indentations along its branches, giving it the appearance of a group of sausages. Growing up to two feet long, the sausage alga also attaches to rocks in the lower intertidal zone. The alga grows through repeated cell divisions and its presence is temperature dependent, not seen during the warm months.

Petalonia grows in the same habitat and at the same time. *Petalonia* consists of flat narrow blades a few inches long. Though this brown alga looks like a small piece of kelp, it lacks the large root-like holdfast or the distinct midrib.

Are there any epiphytic seaweeds?

An epiphyte is a plant growing on or attached to another. There are several seaweeds that are epiphytic. The sea potato (*Leathesia difformis*) is often found attached to Irish moss (*Chondrus crispus*) or eelgrass (*Zostera marina*). One of the red algae species, *Polysiphonia linosa*, is attached only to the brown alga knotted wrack (*Ascophyllum nodosum*). Another common epiphyte is *Ceramium rubrum*, a branching red alga that can be identified by bands along its axes and small tiny claw-like tips. A close examination of most large seaweeds with a hand lens will reveal many different epiphytic algae.

How are seaweeds used in agriculture?

Various seaweeds are fed on directly by cattle and horses. The kelps such as *Alaria* and *Laminaria* are used to feed farm animals. There are also many harvested marine animals, such as sea urchins, which consume kelp and rockweed. Ground up seaweed is also used as a meal supplement in the feed for animals. Seaweed is applied to crops as a fertilizer and adds valuable nutrients including vitamins and minerals to the soil. This can be either a liquid or solid form. The liquid is more readily absorbed by the roots of plants. This form of "seaweed manure" may include nitrogen, accelerate the aeration of the soil, and prevent harmful pests.

Do small seaweeds have simple life cycles?

Not necessarily. For example one of the most common members of the red algae, *Polysiphonia*, is also one of the most complex in its life cycle. This seaweed is attached to rocks, shells, and other algae in the intertidal zone. Bands of cells called pericentral cells occur along the branches and can be seen with a hand lens. The alga collected in the field is likely the tetrasporophyte stage which releases a series of tetraspores. These germinate into either a male or female gametophyte stage. The male produces the spermatangia and the female forms a structure called a cystocarp that is fertilized by a single spermatium. After this occurs another kind of spore, the carpospore, forms and develops and grows into the tetrasporophyte alga again. So even a tiny seaweed as seen here can exhibit a very complicated life cycle.

Where can some of the smallest seaweeds be found?

Locating small seaweeds requires patience and close examination of shallow waters. There are many tiny, almost obscure, algae which remain hidden under shells or larger seaweeds. I sometimes carry a small bucket with me, collect a clump of macroalgae, and take it back to the lab or classroom for inspection. I then spread the collection into large trays where it can be more closely examined. It's often surprising what can be found floating, hidden, or attached to other plants. As mentioned in a previous question, a tiny red alga called *Ceramium rubrum* is frequently attached to other seaweeds, particularly the green *Codium fragile*. Having access to a microscope will make it much easier for an accurate identification.

What is Irish moss?

Irish moss (*Chondrus crispus*) is a red alga and is not a moss. It grows in large populations and is attached to rocks and the substrate by a small disc-shaped holdfast. This alga is a deeply

red to purple color though it may be yellowish-green if exposed to direct sunlight for long periods of time. The blades are up to four inches long and dichotomously branched (main branches divided into two). It usually grows in the lower portions of the intertidal zone.

Irish moss was a part of the Irish diet during the potato famine and Irish immigrants were the first to harvest it in Massachusetts. A large "mossing" industry developed in Scituate, Massachusetts in the mid-1800s and continued through World War II. The harvesting of Irish moss using long iron rakes was another way of earning a living by the sea. Even today a seaweed pudding is made using Irish moss along with some milk, sugar, salt, and vanilla. The substance carrageenan can be extracted from Irish moss and has many commercial and industrial uses. A partial list includes yogurt, beer, puddings, fruit juice, cake batter, pie fillings, and cottage cheese. This thickening agent prevents ice crystal formation in ice cream. It's also used in some medicines, cosmetics, paints, body lotions, and paper production.

What is the most unusual seaweed?

The answer to this question is really a matter of opinion. Seaweeds exist in all sizes and shapes. They are found in many zones in the ocean. And some species have very complicated life cycles and adaptations. One seaweed that deserves consideration as unusual is *Agarum cribosum*, the sea colander. I call it the Swiss cheese alga because of its unique appearance. This large, conspicuous brown alga is found attached to rocks in cold deeper water, but may also be found in the tidal drift.

The alga consists of a fan-shaped blade up to a foot wide that is riddled with holes. It looks like some herbivore has been munching on it, but the perforations are due to its growth habit and the effects of moving water. More common on a rocky

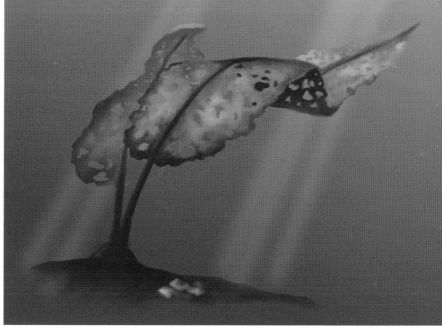

shore, it can also be found near jetties and groins where it attaches with its strong holdfast.

What are the causes and effects of an algae bloom?

Nitrogen acts as a fertilizer and can have a serious impact on the health of aquatic ecosystems. When excess nitrogen runs off into bodies of water a rapid growth of algae called a population bloom may result. This process is called eutrophication. The nitrogen comes from a variety of sources including septic systems, lawn fertilizers, and the atmosphere. When a single species of algae suddenly increases in population, it blocks sunlight to other plants including the ecologically important eelgrass (*Zostera marina*). Bacteria are responsible for the decomposition of the algae. During this process the bacteria use oxygen creating low dissolved oxygen concentrations for invertebrates and fish. Crabs, shrimp, mollusks, and small fish can be killed under these conditions. Some seaweeds, such as sea lettuce (*Ulva lactuca*), can grow in large sheets in such polluted waters. This species can be classified as an environmental indicator for nitrogen loading.

What are the common filamentous green algae growing along the shore?

The most common intertidal filamentous green alga is *Enteromorpha* which has been renamed *Ulva*. The blades of this genus are long, unbranched and often filled with a gas that gives it a swollen appearance. Another green alga in this habitat is *Chaetomorpha* which is wiry and coarse to the touch. Looking like tangled green threads, this seaweed can grow in large mats in tide pools. Finally there is *Cladophora* which is softer and  lighter. This alga is branched and can be more than a foot long. Like other shoreline green algae this genus undergoes a population bloom in the presence of high nitrogen levels.

Can algae be grown on farms?

There are many attempts to grow algae in large concentrations for industrial and agricultural applications. Algae can be used as fertilizers and biofuels. Extracting their important properties is commercially feasible and this field will undoubtedly grow as research continues. Some scientists envision large scale farming or aquacultural enterprises developing to provide food, commercial products, and energy alternatives in a world that increasingly needs these items. At one point it was suggested to grow large seaweed farms in the ocean as a way of reducing the effects of climate change. Some species of seaweed grow very fast and take up carbon dioxide during photosynthesis. Unfortunately many of these same species have a short life span and would release the carbon back into the environment during decomposition. Still the idea of cultivating the algae into other uses while it absorbs carbon dioxide may have some merit.

Algae grown on a small scale has many environmental benefits including the reduction of chemicals, the ability to grow practically anywhere, and the fact that it can be grown throughout the year. If conditions are suitable indoors, such as in a greenhouse, the crop is not limited to any season.

Throughout history, new ways of developing and growing plants for food and other uses take time to become routine. These methods must be economically competitive to be accepted and widely used. But maybe we should try a new approach, one that doesn't require a large corporate presence. Possibly these small scale seaweed farms are preferable. If they can be developed to serve a local need and still be cost effective, then their future could be bright.

What is the relationship between algae and coral?

The ecological roles of algae in the ocean are critical to the sustainability of all life on earth. And any change in the ocean's chemistry or physical structure could have a profound effect on these important organisms. A sudden change in a population suggests the presence of an environmental stressor in its early stages.

Scientists became aware of the problems with climate change when coral reefs showed signs of bleaching. Instead of the bright colors associated with coral animals, the coral turned a skeletal white. This was an indication that they had lost their symbiotic algae called zooxanthellae. A slight change in water temperature can initiate this bleaching phenomenon. The algae provide essential nutrients to the coral so if they don't recover their symbionts, the coral can die. Once that happens the complex coral reef ecosystem can collapse, and many dependent species will perish.

What is the brown seaweed with the small berries that washes up on beaches?

One of the most common brown algae species along the northern Atlantic coastline is *Sargassum*, also called gulf weed. Of all the common seaweeds this one most resembles a true plant. It is easy to confuse the parts of *Sargassum* with those of a plant. But those lance shaped structures that look like leaves are fronds. The berry-like parts along the branch are small air bladders that assist with flotation. The branch itself is a stipe. And while most species of *Sargassum* are planktonic or floating in the water,

the common species on Cape Cod, *Sargassum filipendula*, is attached to rocks by means of a small root-like holdfast.

Sargassum is the seaweed that is floating in huge mats in the Sargasso Sea, a part of the North Atlantic Ocean. The mats are a floating zoo of many different marine animals. Some of these are attached species such as bryozoans and hydroids. Several species of fish swim amongst the seaweed. Animals find shelter and food in these large mats of algae. The air bladders help the algae float, bringing the fronds to the surface to maximize photosynthesis.

Sargassum is considered holopelagic which means it spends its entire life cycle floating in the open ocean. There are several animal species that are endemic or unique to this floating marine habitat. These include crabs, shrimp, and pipefish that specialize in living in and among the fronds of *Sargassum*. The crab's (*Portunas sayi*) appearance even mimics the *Sargassum*, offering it a special form of camouflage.

The floating species of *Sargassum* reproduce vegetatively by a process called fragmentation. The attached species can also reproduce sexually. Male structures called antheridia release motile sperm which fertilize the eggs in the female structure called oogonia. Both of these structures are housed in the conceptacles. Once fertilization is successful, a zygote develops and young gemlings are released that attach to a substrate and grow into an adult.

Like most seaweeds there are many commercial and industrial uses for *Sargassum*. Most marine algae are a good source for iodine and *Sargassum* has been used in alternative medicine to treat goiters. Like other members of the brown algae group, *Sargassum* is also a source of alginate which is used as a stabilizer in many food items and cosmetics. This seaweed has been applied to soil as a conditioner and fertilizer. And in some parts of the world *Sargassum* is consumed directly as a food source.

Are there other kinds of algae in the ocean besides seaweeds?

The phytoplankton are microscopic algae that trap sun energy and kick start the entire marine food web. They are also responsible for the production of most of the earth's oxygen. This group includes the diatoms and the dinoflagellates.

The diatoms are the most abundant group of phytoplankton. They are single-celled and are constructed of two halves, an upper epitheca and a lower hypotheca. They divide frequently, about once every six days. While there is a great diversity of species of diatoms, most of them resemble one of two basic shapes: the cylindrical pennate forms and the circular centric forms. Diatoms are global environmental indicators, often used to study changes in climate and nutrient runoff from land. Because they need sunlight to photosynthesize, they are restricted to the upper portions of the ocean surface where light can penetrate.

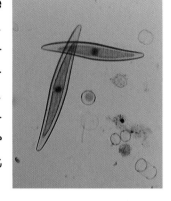

The dinoflagellates are another significant group of phytoplankton. These organisms also possess a pair of flagella which assist in movement. Occasionally they undergo a population explosion or bloom and this can create another problem, depending on the species. *Alexandrium* is a dinoflagellate that is responsible for red tide which usually occurs in the spring. *Alexandrium* contains a neurotoxin that becomes embedded in the tissues of filter-feeding animals such as mollusks. Humans that consume contaminated shellfish can become ill due to paralytic shellfish poisoning. Hence, these shellfish beds are closed until the numbers of plankton cells in the water column are substantially reduced and the mollusks, which are unaffected by the toxic plankton, can feed on other harmless species.

NVS

What are seaweed chips?

Seaweed chips are a healthy alternative to potato chips. Using the edible algae nori (*Porphyra*) and kelp (*Laminaria*), seaweed chips, also called crisps, add fiber to the diet as well as the heart-healthy omega-3 fatty acids. They contain vitamins A, C, and B12. They are high in iodine and calcium. Most seaweed chips are also gluten free with no trans fat or cholesterol. And they contain fewer calories than potato chips. A package of seaweed chips that I examined had 55 calories for 1.2 ounces (35 grams). A bag of potato chips of one ounce (28 grams) had 140 calories. Some companies also add seasonings and the chips are baked instead of fried. The seaweed chips are quite tasty!

Are there any seaweeds that flower?

All seaweeds are algae. Therefore, they do not produce flowers, fruits, or seeds. However, there is a true marine plant that does. Eelgrass (*Zostera marina*) has vascular tissue for the transport of sugars, minerals, and water throughout the plant. The blades grow from a sheath and the plant is attached by a strong root system as well as an underground stem known as a rhizome. It can reproduce both sexually and vegetatively. Eelgrass represents a small ecosystem which includes many animal species such as scallops, blue crabs, flounder, oysters, sea bass, sea urchins, shrimp, and horseshoe crabs. In addition to being a diverse system, eelgrass beds act as buffers to strong wave action. They can contribute to the stability of an area and help protect upland regions from erosion.

What is the sea potato?

An unusually shaped brown seaweed is the sea potato (*Leathesia difformis*). It is also one of the easiest seaweeds to identify, characterized by

being hollow, spherical, and rubbery. It is approximately three to five inches in size, depending on its age. Normally it is found washed up on the beach during the summer months, frequently attached to either eelgrass or Irish moss. It disappears in the winter as it enters its microscopic stage. Its range is from Canada to the Carolinas. The seaweed consists of a mass of thread-like filaments when sectioned and viewed under a microscope.

How are seaweeds distributed along a jetty?

Jetties and groins are often places of attachment for many marine species including seaweeds. Most of the large jetties get periodically bombarded by strong waves and currents. The result is an irregular distribution of plants and animals along the rocks, a phenomenon called patchiness. The movement of water can sweep away the spores and gametes of algae before they get attached. But in those places where a seaweed successfully colonizes a rock surface, a form of zonation can occur.

Near the upper portions of the rock, an area called the splash zone may be slippery due to a blue-green bacterium named *Calothrix*. The presence of this organism gives the rock surface a blackish color.

In general seaweeds follow the pattern in which green algae, most likely *Ulva*, occupy the upper zone followed by the brown seaweeds (*Fucus* and *Ascophyllum*) in the middle zone, and the red algae (*Polysiphonia* and *Chondrus*) in deeper water where their pigments may absorb blue light. If the large seaweeds dominate a rock substrate, their fronds can slide back and forth in the waves preventing the colonization of other species. Rockweeds may also dominate because of their ability to attach to the rock surface with a strong holdfast.

How do some seaweeds avoid freezing during the winter?

Many seaweeds that grow along the upper portions of the shoreline are exposed to a wide variation in temperature. Those species that are present during the winter months in the northeast, such as rockweed, have adapted to these variations. High levels of salts in the exposed fronds lowers the freezing point for the algae. This results in the ability to tolerate much lower temperature before freezing. Those species growing in deeper water are not subject to as wide a range of temperatures as those exposed to the air.

What is a seaweed wrap?

Many spas use seaweed as a body wrap to improve skin tone and remove toxins. The seaweed is usually a paste made from a mixture that includes powdered kelp. Because this seaweed is rich in vitamins and minerals, it is useful by effectively inducing sweating so that toxins and dead skin cells are removed.

Are there any health hazards associated with seaweeds?

When some seaweeds undergo a population bloom, they can quickly pile up on beaches. During decomposition these piles of seaweed are not only unsightly and odorous, but they can release the toxic gas hydrogen sulfide. There are reports of sea lettuce (*Ulva*) and gulf weed (*Sargassum*) causing such problems in many parts of the world. Hydrogen sulfide is so toxic that several beaches have been closed until the noxious seaweed is removed. Most of the time the rotting seaweed is not a serious problem. It is only when the concentrations get too large that a public health hazard may occur.

What is the "killer algae?"

The "killer algae" species is called *Caulerpa taxifolia* and is one of the most invasive species on earth. Appearing first in the Mediterranean Sea, it was originally used in home saltwater aquariums, and was probably accidentally released into the marine environment. Like so many other nuisance species, this one can reproduce quickly. In fact, it can grow a couple of inches a day. It also has the ability to reproduce asexually. Small broken pieces of the fronds can grow into entire plants.

Early warnings were expressed by marine biologist Alexandre Meinesz, but he was largely ignored until the algae had spread over thousands of acres on the ocean floor. *Caulerpa taxifolia* prevents the growth of other, more beneficial, plants by blocking sunlight in the area. It is also quite unpalatable to marine animals because of the toxic compound in its tissues. Once this alga gets  established it becomes an unstoppable monoculture and completely reduces the diversity normally seen. Today it is banned throughout the world as an aquarium plant.

National Oceanic & Atmospheric Administration

What is the seaweed used in clambakes?

Ascophyllum nodosum, commonly called knotted wrack, is one of the largest rockweeds on the east coast and can grow up to three feet long. The fronds are characterized by several large and single air bladders without a distinct midrib. Though *Ascophyllum* is a brown alga, it can have an olive greenish tinge. This seaweed is attached to a hard sub-

strate, such as a rock jetty, by means of a small holdfast. It usually grows from the mid to lower levels of the intertidal zone. A pile of *Ascophyllum* contains enough moisture to provide the steam in cooking clams and vegetables in clambakes. The ability to retain moisture also makes it a suitable packing material for lobsters and other seafood.

Can seaweed be used in a garden?

Gardeners who live near the coastline should take advantage of the seaweeds available. Seaweeds can be used in composting and mulching in a garden. Somewhat low in nitrogen and phosphorous, many seaweeds still contain about 60 trace minerals that benefit the soil by keeping it moist and free from pests

NVS

like slugs and fungi. If you mix the seaweed with existing compost, it's unnecessary to wash the salt from the algae. Collect the drier, crunchier seaweed from the middle of the beach. It breaks up faster, is lighter, and less likely to have attached animals. The use of seaweed in a garden is an effective and natural way of protecting plants.

How are seaweeds classified?

Classification systems frequently change based on new data and information, and seaweeds are no different. However, most scientists recognize three groups based primarily on the different pigments present in the cells of the algae. Botanists call these groups phyla or divisions. The three groups are green (Chlorophyta), brown (Phaeophyta), and red (Rhodophyta) algae. Technically seaweeds are not true plants.

GDN

They lack the specialized tissues for the transport of food and water. Instead of the kingdom Plantae, the seaweeds are placed in the kingdom Protista.

Who is the "Mother of the Sea"?

Smithsonian Instutituion Archives

Dr. Kathleen Drew-Baker was a phycologist (scientist who studies algae) at the University of Manchester in England. Dr. Drew-Baker's specialty was red algae; she successfully identified a critical stage in the life cycle of *Porphyra umbilicalis* which is the nori widely used in sushi. She showed that there is a microscopic stage called the Conchocelis that is attached to shells. The discovery of this phase had enormous economic implications which allowed nori farmers to improve the success at which they grew the seaweed. Consequently there is a shrine in Japan in Dr. Drew-Baker's honor and she is today referred to as the "Mother of the Sea."

What is the life cycle of rockweed?

Rockweed (*Fucus vesiculosus*) is common on the banks of salt marshes, jetties, pilings and other hard surfaces. The brown, forked branches have pairs of small air bladders along the midrib of the frond which help the alga float in the water. Sometimes the tips are swollen with small bumps that contain the reproductive conceptacles. The male conceptacles contain structures called antheridia which release motile sperm cells in the water when the tide comes in. The female conceptacles contain structures called oogonia which release the egg cells that are carried by water currents. A single sperm cell fertilizes an egg cell and the resulting zygote settles down on a solid surface. It then grows into a new rockweed alga.

Is the holdfast similar to a root?

Most seaweeds need a point of attachment to a strong object or the substrate to resist removal by wave energy. Because seaweeds do not have roots, this is accomplished by a structure called a holdfast. Unlike roots, holdfasts do not transport materials throughout the alga, but function only as anchorage. A holdfast has specialized branched tissues called haptera which attach to an object. Depending on the substrate, there are different kinds of holdfasts. For example, kelp is attached to rocks by means of a very strong, root-shaped holdfast. On the other hand, sea lettuce, which grows in quieter, shallower areas, is attached by a small disk-shaped holdfast.

What are calcifying seaweeds?

Several species of seaweeds, particularly in the tropics, have the ability to remove limestone (calcium carbonate) from the water and deposit it on their fronds. Some of the common tropical calcifying species include the green alga *Halimeda*, the brown alga *Padina*, and the red coralline algae. In northern waters the coral weed (*Corallina officinalis*) is commonly found, frequently growing on the shells of periwinkle snails.

When alive, *Corallina* is pink to purple in color, but it bleaches white when it dies. The alga is jointed with flexible areas free from lime deposits. This allows it to move back and forth in the waves without breaking. It can grow up to six inches in length and has a small disc-shaped holdfast that attaches to solid objects. Most scientists believe that enough light penetrates the limestone encrusted surface to allow photosynthesis to take place. And possibly the limestone coating discourages animals from grazing on the soft tissues, although sea urchins, which need lime for the construction of their shells, may consume the coralline algae.

Do seaweeds cause red tide?

Red tide is caused by a marine harmful algal bloom, but the culprit is not a seaweed. Instead, it is one of the microalgae in a group called the dinoflagellates. Northeastern red tides are due to a population bloom of the dinoflagellate *Alexandrium*. The waters do not turn red, nor is this related to tides. However, *Alexandrium* contains a neurotoxin which becomes embedded in the tissues of mollusks as they filter feed the tiny organism. Humans are vulnerable to a disease called paralytic shellfish poisoning (PSP) should they consume shellfish at that time. This is rarely fatal, but it can make one quite ill. Government officials often close shellfish beds during this outbreak of red tide. Eventually the dinoflagellate population decreases and the concentration of toxin in shellfish tissues declines, so it becomes safe to consume the shellfish again.

What is the prettiest seaweed?

The prettiest seaweed is, of course, a matter of opinion. However, one of the candidates has to be the filamentous red alga chenille weed (*Dasya pedicellata*). This warm water seaweed appears as a finely branched and delicate bright red form under water. It can be found detached and floating in bays and estuaries. Examine it with a hand lens and you will observe many tiny hairs along  the branches. The alga is soft to the touch and collapses when removed from the water. Chenille weed makes an excellent pressed specimen and, if done properly, will retain its bright red color and shape for many years.

What is miso soup?

Miso is a tasty soup that is common in Japan. It contains the seaweeds kelp or nori. The soup is prepared with a stock called dashi and a fermented miso paste. Tofu and various vegetables are also added to this nutritious soup that is low in calories and high in protein. Miso soup is considered a healthy food item because it can help you lose weight by suppressing your appetite and assisting in digestion. There are many different recipes for miso soups, varying in the kinds of ingredients added.

Jim Brown

Who was William Randolph Taylor?

Dr. William Randolph Taylor (1895-1990) was a professor of botany at the University of Michigan. He was the curator of algae there and wrote two definitive identification keys for marine algae in the northeast and the tropics. The books are *Marine Algae of the Northeastern Coast of North America* and *Marine Algae of the Eastern Tropical and Subtropical Coasts of the Americas*. Both books have been used by students of phycology for many years. Dr. Taylor also taught summer marine algae classes at the Marine Biological Laboratory in Woods Hole, Massachusetts. His books remain classics in the study of seaweeds throughout these regions.

What is phycology?

Phycology is a specialization in the field of botany that involves the scientific study of algae. This not only includes the seaweeds, but also the abundant microalgae and all freshwater species. While algae have been studied for centuries, many believe that the earliest influential phycologist was William Henry Harvey (1811-1866) from Ireland. Harvey divided the algae into groups based on their color or pigmentation, a classification system still in effect today, though other characteristics are also used to distinguish algae divisions. Like Charles Darwin, William Harvey traveled to other parts of the world, collected many specimens, and described hundreds of species. He wrote several books including the classics *Phycologia Australia* and *A Manual of the British Algae*. Today there are several professional phycology organizations throughout the world including the Phycological Society of America, founded in 1946, which publishes the *Journal of Phycology*.

NVS

Does seaweed taste like bacon?

Researchers at the Oregon State University have patented a strain of dulse that tastes like bacon when fried. Dulse is a red seaweed called *Palmaria palmata*. And, like many other seaweeds, it is very nutritious, rich in vitamins, iodine and other minerals. It can be eaten in a raw or dried form. It grows in deeper water attached to rocks and shells and prefers a rocky shoreline. The blades are reddish-purple and shaped like a flattened fan. The scientists who developed this new strain were looking to feed abalone, but discovered that it can be quite tasty to humans as well.

What is the seaweed in seaweed salad?

The most commonly used seaweed in a seaweed salad is a brown alga called wakame. There are two closely related brown algae species that are used as wakame. In Japan and Korea the seaweed grown is *Undaria pinnatifida*, whereas in the United States it's *Alaria esculenta*. These seaweeds are sometimes called winged kelps because they have specialized reproductive blades called sporophylls in a cluster at the base of the stipe. Both of these species are rich in omega-3 fatty acid, vitamins and minerals. Commercial seaweed salads are available in grocery stores and are sold throughout the world.

NVS

How many species of seaweeds are there?

It's not that easy to give an exact number of species because the taxonomy frequently changes and new data on life cycles and genetics continues to accumulate. Most estimates suggest there are about 7,000-8,000 species of green algae, most of these in freshwater. Between 10-15% are marine. However, it's a different picture with the brown algae. Nearly 99% of the 1,500-2,000 species are in the ocean. The red algae are also more common in marine waters, having 98% of the 5,000-6,000 species.

What is seaweed pudding?

Seaweed pudding is a sweet dessert made from the red alga Irish moss (*Chondrus crispus*). It is boiled with milk, strained, and then combined with sugar, honey, salt, and cream. As it thickens, various fruits can be added such as blueberries, strawberries and even coconuts. Some recipes call for use of vanilla extract. Like so many other seaweed recipes, this one is also nutritious and delicious.

Can seaweeds play a role in reducing the effects of climate change?

Marine algae, like true plants, have the ability to photosynthesize, a process that takes in carbon dioxide and releases oxygen. Because carbon dioxide is a greenhouse gas, many believe that encouraging the growth of seaweed could help alleviate the effects of climate change. For example, large kelp farms and forests could be cultivated to absorb the carbon dioxide. Kelp can then be harvested for various commercial products. Of course the carbon is released back into the environment when the seaweed is used or decomposes. Possibly the seaweed could be used as a biofuel, offseting the consumption of fossil fuels.

What is the function of the air bladders?

Several brown algae species such as the rockweeds and kelps may contain air or gas bladders for flotation. These structures are also called pneumatocysts. In the common rockweed, *Fucus vesiculosus*, the air bladders are in pairs along the midrib. In the larger kelps they exist nearer the tips of the algae. In all cases this enables the fronds to float closer to the surface thus maximizing their ability to photosynthesize. That is why one shouldn't pop them at the beach! The air bladders contain the gases carbon dioxide, nitrogen and oxygen – just like the atmosphere. Some kelps may even contain a small amount of carbon monoxide.

What is the seaweed with the "lobster claws"?

One of the prettiest seaweeds is a small, bushy red alga called *Ceramium rubrum*. This species grows in tide pools, quiet bays, and in the intertidal zone attached to rocks. The tips fork inward like tiny claws hence the common description of having "lobster claws". These are easily seen with a hand lens. The bushy branches consist of tiny red bands that encircle the main axis. The alga can appear in clumps, pieces along the beach, or attached to larger seaweeds. Look for these "claws" at the tips as this species can sometimes be confused with *Polysiphonia*, another red alga which is missing that characteristic.

What are the different pigments that give seaweeds their unique colors?

All three groups of seaweeds contain the pigment chlorophyll which is used in photosynthesis. However, the brown algae also contain two groups of pigments called carotenoids and xanthophylls. These tend to mask the green chlorophyll. The rockweeds contain one of these pigments called fucoxanthin which gives the characteristic brown color.

The **red** algae contain phycobilin pigments which also mask the chlorophyll. This set of pigments includes phycoerythrin, a common pigment that absorbs blue light and helps the red algae colonize deeper depths.

What is meant by an alternation of generations?

The life cycles of algae may have two distinct stages. One stage has twice the number of chromosomes and is called the diploid sporophyte which releases the spores. The other has half the number of chromosomes and is called the haploid gametophyte which releases the female and male gametes. These stages rotate with each other and may even be free-standing, as seen in sea lettuce. Thus, it is referred to as an alternation of generations.

Should seaweed be harvested as packing material for the shipment of clams and lobsters?

The removal of any seaweed along the shoreline can have an impact on many other species. The most common seaweed used in packing is rockweed, including both *Ascophyllum* and *Fucus.* Rockweed protects animals, such as lobsters and clams, from desiccation and predators. These predators include periwinkles, sea urchins, and other common invertebrates. Other tiny animals and some algae attach to rockweed. For example, the tube worm *Spirorbus* is often seen on *Fucus vesiculosus.* Even larger animals, including several species of fish and ducks, will  seek food in the rockweed. Though these algae are commercially important for many products, care should be used when removing them. It's important not to create a barren habitat where numerous species may be ecologically significant.

What is the sea whip?

The sea whip is the brown alga *Chorda filum*, also called the sea lace. This unusual seaweed is a long, dark brown, whip-shaped alga that is attached to rocks or shells by a small flat holdfast. The sea whip is in the kelp group, although it looks 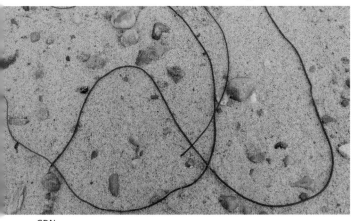 quite different from its relatives. *Chorda* appears in the summer and grows in deeper water, often in clumps. It feels smooth when handled and is unbranched. Some specimens may be greater than fifteen feet long.

GDN

What is the best way to collect and preserve seaweeds?

Examine any sample of seaweed before you collect it. Remove any small animals and check to see if you have an undamaged whole alga. Collect it in seawater and prepare a pressed specimen as soon as you get it home.

Float the alga in a tray with seawater. Place a thick piece of paper (herbarium stock if available) under the specimen. Raise the paper so that the seaweed is on top and drain the water. You can also arrange the alga the way you want it pressed by using a medicine dropper or forceps. Cover the alga with wax paper or cheese cloth and place it between a set of newspapers. Put some heavy books on top and change the newspaper the next day. The paper will absorb the residual water.

After 2-3 days you can peel off the covering on the seaweed. The specimen should stick to the herbarium paper. The most successful pressed specimens are those that have been dried properly. The alga can retain its color for several years if done correctly.

This process works best for thin filamentous algae. The thicker, heavier species may need to be glued to the paper after the drying process. Some of these are better preserved in a commercial solution of formalin.

For step-by-step procedure, see
Activity: The Seaweed Herbarium
on page 37

Are seaweeds in the tropical region different from those in temperate waters?

The tropics have a wide diversity of marine algae species, several not found in colder temperate waters. One of the major differences I found when studying the two areas was the more common ability to calcify in warmer waters. Some tropical species that calcified included *Penicillus*, *Halimeda*, and *Udotea*. Many calcareous algae have an important role in the formation of the sensitive coral reefs. The algae there resemble small statues under the water. My favorite warm water species is the brown alga *Padina vickersiae* with its fan-shaped blades in clusters in shallow waters.

What are blue green algae?

The blue-green algae are photosynthetic bacteria that are classified as the Cyanophyta or cyanobacteria. Their cell structure is much simpler than that of the macroalgae or seaweeds. There are no organized nuclei. The pigments are scattered and not in specialized organelles. Cells reproduce by dividing, resulting in a filamentous structure. One of the most common species is *Calothrix crustacea* which appears as blackish patches on the surface of intertidal rocks. Because it is difficult to see the alga, it creates a slippery surface on the rocks. Some blue-green algae are very toxic. Some have the ability to fix nitrogen into useable forms much like the bacteria in the root nodules of legume plants.

Why is the holdfast of the giant kelp considered to be another habitat?

The holdfast of the giant kelp (*Macrocystis pyrifera*) off the California coast attaches the large alga to rock surfaces. Though it can be dislodged during storms and strong currents, it is very effective at keeping the seaweed from breaking away. A large number of animal species are often found here, including several echinoderms, worms, crabs, amphipods, and mollusks. It is also a location for many animal species to lay their eggs and seek shelter from predators.

Is it a sign of pollution to find a large amount of seaweed on a beach?

There are several reasons why a beach may contain a large population of seaweed. Strong currents, wave action, and storms can result in piles of seaweed along the shore. If an area has large rocks or jetties, then these become places of attachment for some algae. Nitrogen loading can lead to a population bloom of a single species of algae such as the green *Ulva* and 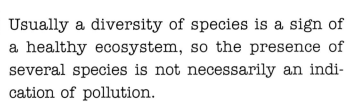 *Cladophora* or the red *Gracilaria*.

Usually a diversity of species is a sign of a healthy ecosystem, so the presence of several species is not necessarily an indication of pollution.

Can the presence of seaweed prevent erosion?

When seaweeds pile up on a beach, they trap sand particles from the wind and can help stabilize the area. If this continues over time, a small berm may form with mats of decomposing seaweed as a sand covered base. Subtidal populations of seaweed, particularly in a kelp forest, may impede strong currents and waves from reaching the shore at full capacity. Also the banks of salt marshes are frequently colonized by an extensive population of rockweed which helps prevent erosion in the marsh.

What is the seaweed that has tiny hooks?

This seaweed is called *Hypnea musciformis* and is a member of the red algae. Southern Massachusetts represents its most northern distribution, but it is quite common in the tropics. The branches are unmistakable as they contain tiny hooks on the tips. *Hypnea* is found mainly in sheltered and shallow areas where the water may be warmer. This alga has many branches and can be greater than a foot long. Like many species, it is attached to rocks in its habitat.

What are the bluish-green lights seen in the water after dark?

These lights are a form of bioluminescence, most likely caused by an algae bloom of microscopic phytoplankton called dinoflagellates. Some of these species are responsible for red tide. The lights are usually seen if the water is in motion. An enzyme called luciferin reacts with oxygen and gives off the light without heat. Many other marine organisms are bioluminescent including some jellyfish and several species of deep sea fish.

Are there any seaweeds considered to be threatened or endangered?

It doesn't appear that there are any seaweeds in northeast North America that are threatened or endangered. However, because of the increase in invasive species and the predominance of algae blooms due to nitrogen loading, the diversity of species in an area is often reduced.

One marine plant species, Johnson's seagrass (*Halophilia johnsonii*), was listed as threatened in 1999. And there are many places where eel grass (*Zostera marina*) populations have severly declined because of surface algae blooms blocking essential sunlight to the deeper water grasses.

ACTIVITY

THE SEAWEED HERBARIUM

There is an easy and fun way to pre-serve seaweeds for study and use. Creating a seaweed herbarium allows the beachcomber to collect various species at different seasons and to press them so that they last for several years.

1. Acquire the following materials:
   a. a tray at least one inch deep
   b. cheese cloth or wax paper
   c. paper made of a thick stock
   d. newspapers
   e. scissors
   f. bucket to carry seaweeds
   g. several heavy books

2. Collect whole specimens of seaweeds that have not been bleached or decomposed.

3. Transport the seaweed back home in a bucket of salt water.

4. Put some of the seawater in the tray and float the seaweed on top.

5. Cut a section of thick paper and place it in the water under the seaweed.

6. Slowly raise the paper and gently arrange the seaweed the way you want it pressed. A small medicine dropper can help you arrange any fine filaments.

7. Carefully remove the paper and drain the excess water off the sides.

8. Cut a section of cheese cloth or wax paper and cover the seaweed. The cheese cloth works better as the seaweed is less likely to stick to it.

9. Gently tap on this covering.

10. Place the specimen between a couple of sheets of newspaper and close.

11. Place some heavy books on the newspaper.

12. Change the newspaper each day for a couple of days. This helps absorb any moisture.

13. After a couple of days carefully peel the cheese cloth off the specimen. The seaweed should stick to the paper.

14. You can combine different species in the same paper.

15. Please note that this process works best for fine, fila-mentous algae, but is difficult for thick or large seaweeds.

ACTIVITY

EXAMINING ROCKWEED

The common rockweed (*Fucus vesiculosus*) grows in the muddy banks of salt marshes as well as on jetties, pilings, and other hard surfaces. The brown forked branches have pairs of small air bladders along the midrib of the frond which help the alga float in the water. The alga is attached to the substrate by a root-like holdfast. The swollen tips  are called receptacles and contain the reproductive cells.

1. Locate a population of rockweed at low tide and describe its habitat.

2. Is the alga growing in extensive clumps or is it distributed randomly in this area?

3. Identify the following structures:
    a. frond
    b. air bladders
    c. holdfast
    d. receptacle
    e. midrib

4. How are the air bladders arranged along the midrib?

5. Do you see small bumps on the receptacles? If so, these are the conceptacles and contain the male and female reproductive cells.

6. Carefully lift a clump of rockweed without removing it from the substrate.

7. Do you see any of the following animals: ribbed mussels, barnacles, sand hoppers, or attached bryozoans?

8. Why are these animals living underneath the rockweed?

9. Use a hand lens and look carefully at the rockweed branches.

10. Do you see a small curly white case attached to the fronds? This is the tube worm *Spirorbus*.

11. Are there any other animals attached such as barnacles?

12. Are there any smaller seaweeds attached such as different species of red algae?

13. Even though rockweed is brown, it is a producer and makes its own food through the process of photosynthesis. How do the air bladders help this process?

14. Are there other seaweeds in this habitat?

15. Why are different kinds of rockweeds, particularly the knotted wrack (*Ascophyllum nodosum*), used as packing material for clams and lobsters?

ACKNOWLEDGEMENTS

I am very grateful to the following individuals
for their assistance and support:

To **Chris Dumas** whose excellent photography and illustrations
enhance this book.

To **Nancy Viall Shoemaker** for her continuing professional
advice and guidance in the design and creation of all my
books - as well as her photographs. I was pleased to have
Nancy write the Foreword for this publication.

RECOMMENDED SEAWEED READINGS

Dawson, E. Yale. *Marine Botany*. Holt, Rinehart, and Winston. New York. 1966.

Druehl, Louis D. *Pacific Seaweeds*. Harbour Publishing. Canada. 2007.

Kingsbury, John M. *Seaweeds of Cape Cod and the Islands.* The Chatham Press, Inc. Chatham, Massachusetts. 1969.

McConnaughey, Evelyn M. *Sea Vegetables*. Naturegraph Publishers, Inc. California. 2009.

Meinesz, Alexandre. *Killer Algae*. University of Chicago Press. Chicago, Illinois. 1999.

Newton, Gilbert D. *Seaweeds of Cape Cod Shores*. West Barnstable Press, Massachusetts. 2008.

Taylor, William Randolph. *Marine Algae of the Northeastern Coast of North America.* University of Michigan Press, Michigan. 1957.

Treat, Rose. *The Seaweed Book*. Star Bright Books. New York. 1995.

ABOUT THE AUTHOR

Gilbert Newton is a Cape Cod native who has been teaching environmental and marine science at Sandwich High School and Cape Cod Community College for many years. His classes included coastal ecology, botany, coastal zone management, and environmental technology. In 2013 he became the first Director of the Sandwich STEM Academy. Gil has also taught classes for Massachusetts Maritime Academy, Falmouth Academy, Bridgewater State University, and Waquoit Bay National Estuarine Research Reserve. He was the Program Director for the Advanced Studies and Leadership Program at Massachusetts Maritime Academy for 14 years.

Gil is one of the founders of the Barnstable Land Trust and is the past president of the Association to Preserve Cape Cod. He completed his graduate work in biology at Florida State University. Gil is the author of several books about the Cape's shoreline including the recent *Marine Habitats of Cape Cod*.

ABOUT THE PHOTOGRAPHER

Chris Dumas has lived and worked on Cape Cod for many years. He teaches earth and space science at Sandwich High School and is an advisor to the photography club there. Chris has been involved with outdoor education for most of his career. Photography has been an important part of Chris' life for the last decade. He has traveled around the country in search of interesting vistas. Chris has a graduate degree in Resource Conservation from the University of Montana and is a native of the St. Lawrence River region of New York. His photography can also be seen in *The Ecology of a Cape Cod Salt Marsh*, *Discovering the Cape Cod Shoreline*, *Coastal Corners of Cape Cod*, and *Marine Habitats of Cape Cod*.

BOOKS BY GILBERT NEWTON

Seaweeds of Cape Cod Shores

The Ecology of a Cape Cod Salt Marsh

Discovering the Cape Cod Shoreline

Coastal Corners of Cape Cod

Marine Habitats of Cape Cod

All books are published by West Barnstable Press.

This book was designed and typeset by West Barnstable Press, www.westbarnstablepress.com. The font used for the title is a playful 1960s favorite, **Ad Lib**, which was designed by Freeman Craw for American Type Founders in 1994. The text font is **American Typewriter**, built by Joel Kaden and Tony Stan for International Typeface Corp. in 1974. It is a nod to manual typewriters but, unlike those vintage producers of type, the font has proportional sizing (all letters are not the same width). Photo credits were set in **Frutiger**, designed by Swiss typographer Adrian Frutiger (1928-2015). *Mysteries of Seaweed, Questions and Answers* was printed on 100 lb. white matte stock with a 12 pt. laminated cover.

Printed on recycled paper ♲